THE REAL
Edith Wilson

Virginia Loh-Hagan

45th Parallel Press

Published in the United States of America by Cherry Lake Publishing
Ann Arbor, Michigan
www.cherrylakepublishing.com

Reading Adviser: Marla Conn MS, Ed., Literacy specialist, Read-Ability, Inc.
Book Cover Design: Felicia Macheske

Photo Credits: © Library of Congress/C.M. Bell [1886-1896]/Reproduction No. LC-DIG-ds-01086, Cover, 1, 15; © Library of Congress/Reproduction No. LC-USZ62-25808, 5, 30; © Library of Congress/Harris & Ewing [June 1920]/Reproduction No. LC-DIG-ppmsca-13425, 7; © Library of Congress/Reproduction No. LC-USZ62-22737, 9; © Library of Congress/Reproduction No. LC-DIG-anrc-01194, 11; © pg 12 TK; © ArtMarie/iStock, 17; © Library of Congress/Harris & Ewing [1915]/Reproduction No. LC-DIG-hec-06261, 19; © Library of Congress/Reproduction No. LC-DIG-npcc-24212, 20; © Library of Congress/Bain News Service [publisher]/Reproduction No. LC-DIG-ggbain-03388, 23; © Library of Congress/Harris & Ewing [1913]/Reproduction No. LC-DIG-hec-02333, 24; © Library of Congress/Harris & Ewing [1914]/Reproduction No. LC-DIG-hec-04151, 27; © Library of Congress/Harris & Ewing [April 14, 1936]/Reproduction No. LC-DIG-hec-40582, 29

Graphic Elements Throughout: © iulias/Shutterstock.com; © Thinglass/Shutterstock.com; © kzww/Shutterstock.com; © A_Lesik/Shutterstock.com; © MegaShabanov/Shutterstock.com; © Groundback Atelier/Shutterstock.com; © saki80/Shutterstock.com

Copyright © 2019 by Cherry Lake Publishing
All rights reserved. No part of this book may be reproduced or utilized in any form or by any means without written permission from the publisher.

45th Parallel Press is an imprint of Cherry Lake Publishing.

Library of Congress Cataloging-in-Publication Data

Names: Loh-Hagan, Virginia, author.
Title: The Real Edith Wilson / by Virginia Loh-Hagan.
Description: Ann Arbor, Michigan : Cherry Lake Publishing, [2019]. | Series: History uncut | Includes bibliographical references and index.
Identifiers: LCCN 2018035189 | ISBN 9781534143340 (hardcover) | ISBN 9781534141100 (pdf) | ISBN 9781534139909 (pbk.) | ISBN 9781534142305 (hosted ebook)
Subjects: LCSH: Wilson, Edith Bolling Galt, 1872-1961—Juvenile literature. | Presidents' spouses—United States—Biography—Juvenile literature
Classification: LCC E767.3 .L64 2019 | DDC 973.91/3092 [B]—dc23
LC record available at https://lccn.loc.gov/2018035189

Cherry Lake Publishing would like to acknowledge the work of The Partnership for 21st Century Skills. Please visit www.p21.org for more information.

Printed in the United States of America
Corporate Graphics

Table of Contents

Chapter 1
Edith Wilson
The Story You Know 4

Chapter 2
Secret President 6

Chapter 3
War Heroine 10

Chapter 4
Famous Family 14

Chapter 5
Modern Woman 18

Chapter 6
The Second Mrs. Wilson 22

Chapter 7
Wilson vs. Suffragettes 26

Timeline 30

Consider This! 31
Learn More 31
Glossary 32
Index 32
About the Author 32

CHAPTER 1

Edith Wilson
The Story You Know

Edith Wilson was the wife of a U.S. president. She was a **First Lady**. This is the title of a male president's wife. Wilson was married to President Woodrow Wilson. He was the 28th U.S. president. He's famous for leading the country into World War I. He wanted to make the world "safe for **democracy**." Democracy means government by the people.

Mrs. Wilson supported her husband. She was a good wife. She was a good American. She showed that women could be world leaders. She paved the way for other women. But there's more to her story …

Mrs. Wilson was the first First Lady to get Secret Service protection.

CHAPTER 2

Secret President

Edith Wilson was much more than the First Lady. Some people think she was the first female president. She never left President Wilson's side. She worked with him in his private office. She read his top-secret papers. She had his top-secret wartime codes. She read his mail. She went to his meetings.

Then, President Wilson had a **stroke**. Strokes are like brain attacks. This happened in 1919. President Wilson had to stay in bed. He couldn't move some of his body parts.

Mrs. Wilson took over. She kept the president's sickness a secret. She wouldn't let him quit. She told people he needed rest.

Mrs. Wilson was called a First Lady president.

SETTING THE WORLD STAGE
1872

- Yellowstone National Park became the world's first national park. It's located in Wyoming, Montana, and Idaho. President Ulysses S. Grant signed a law to protect the park. This means nobody can build on park lands. The lands belong to nature. They're for everyone to enjoy. National parks are known as "America's best idea."

- **Mary Celeste** was a ship. It's known as a ghost ship. It set sail in 1872. It disappeared. Everyone on the ship disappeared as well. No one knows what happened. Some people think pirates attacked. Some think aliens kidnapped the crew. Some think there was a storm at sea. Some think there was a fiery explosion.

- Victoria Woodhull became the first woman to run for U.S. president. She was in the Equal Rights Party. She was known as a freethinker. She created her own newspaper. She fought for women's rights.

"I had three brothers. Two died early. And one of them was living a good long time." — Edith Wilson

She helped him manage the country. She read all his papers. She decided what and who the president should see or not see. She took news to him. She had him sign things. She delivered messages to and from him. She went to his meetings.

Mrs. Wilson denied being president. She said she was a **steward**. Stewards are caregivers. Mrs. Wilson said she never made any decisions.

Mrs. Wilson was the secret president for close to 2 years.

CHAPTER 3

War Heroine

Most First Ladies are **hostesses**. This means they plan parties. They host events. They entertain guests. Mrs. Wilson was First Lady during World War I. During the war, life changed. Men were sent away to fight. The war cost a lot of money. There wasn't much food. There weren't as many things. People had to **ration**. Ration means to save. Mrs. Wilson didn't waste money hosting events. She didn't host White House tours.

She set an example. She didn't use gas on Sundays. She didn't eat meat on Mondays. She didn't eat wheat on Wednesdays. She encouraged others to do the same. People rationed because the war caused **shortages**. A shortage is a lack of something.

Mrs. Wilson hired a secretary to take care of her social events.

The White House has a lawn. Lawns need to be cut. Usually, men do this work. But men were busy fighting. So, Mrs. Wilson brought in 48 sheep. She had the sheep eat the grass. Then, she had the sheep's wool cut off. She sold the wool. She raised money. She gave the money to the American Red Cross.

She did a lot to help the war. She knitted hats for soldiers. She sewed pillowcases and blankets. She wrote letters to soldiers. She planned **war bond** parties. War bonds are certificates that act like money. People would buy these certificates. The money raised was given to the government. It was used to pay for the war.

Mrs. Wilson raised over $50,000 from selling the wool.

THAT Happened?!?

There's a play about Edith Wilson. It's called *The Second Mrs. Wilson*. It's about how Mrs. Wilson took over for President Wilson. It's written by Joe DiPietro. DiPietro was inspired by an article. The article was about female politicians. It said that Hillary Clinton wouldn't be the first female president. It mentioned Mrs. Wilson. DiPietro thought that was interesting. He did research. He said, "This is an unbelievable story about a woman that is essentially running the country at a time when women couldn't even vote!" He was surprised that more people didn't know about her. Mrs. Wilson's character is the only woman in the play.

"I am not thinking of the country now. I am thinking of my husband." — Edith Wilson

CHAPTER 4

Famous Family

Edith was born in 1872. She was born in Virginia. Her parents were William and Sarah Bolling. The Bollings had 11 children. Edith was the seventh child.

The Bollings were **descendants** of early Virginia settlers. Descendants are people related to people who lived in the past. Edith's father was related to Pocahontas and John Rolfe. Pocahontas was a famous Native American.

Edith's great-grandmother was Thomas Jefferson's sister. Jefferson was the third U.S. president. Edith was also related to Martha Washington. Washington was the first U.S. president's wife. Another relation was Robert E. Lee. Lee was a general in the U.S. Civil War.

Some people said Edith was a "real American princess of [Native American] lineage."

All in the Family

Pocahontas was born around 1596. She was Native American. She was part of the Powhatan tribe. She lived around the Chesapeake Bay area. She was the chief's daughter. She was named Amonute. But she's known as Pocahontas. This means "playful one." English people came to Virginia. They came in the early 1600s. Captain John Smith was captured by the chief's brother. He was about to be killed. But Pocahontas saved his life. She helped the English settle. She delivered messages. She gave food to the English. But the English wanted more. The Powhatans didn't have any more. There was a battle. Pocahontas stopped helping. She was kidnapped by an English captain. She was taken to Richmond. She met John Rolfe. She married him. Their marriage was known as the "peace of Pocahontas." They had a son named Thomas. Pocahontas died in 1617.

"I will be ready to be mustered in as soon as can be." — Edith Wilson

The Bollings were very rich before the Civil War. Then, they lost their money and their home. So, even though Edith had famous family members, she grew up poor. She lived in a crowded house.

The Bollings sent the boys to school. They didn't have much money to educate the girls. Edith only went to school for 2 years. She mostly learned at home. She took care of her sick grandmother, Anne Bolling. She also took care of her 26 pet birds. Her grandmother taught her to read and write. She taught her to speak French. She taught her to sew. She taught her music and poetry. She taught her to be a strong woman.

Edith lived with her family, plus two grandmothers, several aunts, and some cousins.

CHAPTER 5

Modern Woman

Edith met Norman Galt. She married him in 1896. This was before she met President Wilson. Galt owned a jewelry store. He sold gold. He sold silver. His shop had been around since Lincoln's time.

Edith and Galt lived in Washington, D.C., for 12 years. They had one son. The son only lived a few days. Edith had a hard time giving birth. She wasn't able to have more children.

Galt spent money on Edith. He bought her fancy clothes. He bought her jewelry. He took her out to fancy dinners. He took her to plays. He also helped her family.

Galt took over the jewelry store from his grandfather in 1891.

In 1904, she got a driver's **license**. Licenses are permits. Edith learned how to drive a car. She was the first woman in her city to do this. She could go wherever she wanted. Her car could travel 13 miles (21 kilometers) per hour. It was worth about $44,000. It was very modern for its time.

Galt died in 1908. This left Edith a rich woman. She took over the business. She traveled a lot. She liked the fashion in Paris. She was unlike most women of her time. She had her own money. And she had a lot of freedom.

Edith was a tall woman at 5 feet 9 inches (1.75 meters).

Bad Blood

Mrs. Wilson blamed Henry Cabot Lodge for her husband's stroke. Lodge was against President Wilson's ideas. He said bad things about the president. He led people to vote against the president. This stressed out President Wilson. Lodge was the Republican leader of the Senate. He was from Massachusetts. His family was rich. They owned shipping companies. Lodge was born in 1850. He went to Harvard. He earned the first doctorate in political science. He taught at Harvard. He taught American history. He became a politician. He ran for various offices. He was a senator for over 30 years. He said, "The United States is the world's best hope." He didn't want to get too involved with other countries' problems. He disagreed with President Wilson's League of Nations. He didn't want to be part of it. He died in 1924. He had a stroke. He died 9 months after President Wilson.

"He must never know how ill he was, and I must carry on." — Edith Wilson

CHAPTER 6

The Second Mrs. Wilson

One of Edith's best friends was Altrude Gordon. Gordon was dating Cary Grayson. Grayson was the White House doctor.

President Wilson was also a **widower**. Widowers are men whose spouse or partner died. President Wilson's cousin moved into the White House. Her name was Helen Woodrow Bones. She helped him host events.

Gordon and Edith went on a hike. Bones joined them. She invited them to the White House for tea. That's how Edith and President Wilson met. President Wilson fell in love. It was the first time he had laughed since his first wife died. President Wilson was very romantic. He sent her flowers. He wrote her many love letters. He signed them from "Tiger."

Ellen Wilson, the first Mrs. Wilson, was First Lady for only 17 months!

Three months later in 1915, he asked her to marry him. His advisers didn't want him to do it. They tried to push Edith away. They were afraid he'd lose his reelection. They thought it was too soon after his first wife's death. But his first wife had told Grayson to tell the president to marry again.

President Wilson asked Edith if she wanted to get out of marrying him. She said she'd stand by him for love, not duty. Edith became the second Mrs. Wilson.

◀ Mrs. Wilson fired people she didn't like.

CHAPTER 7

Wilson vs. Suffragettes

Not everyone loved the First Lady. One U.S. leader said she "fulfilled the dream of the **suffragettes** by changing her title from First Lady to Acting First Man." Suffragettes were women who fought for voting rights for women. This comment was meant to hurt Mrs. Wilson.

Mrs. Wilson was a strong female leader. It would make sense for her to fight for women's voting rights. But she didn't. She didn't support suffragettes. She blamed them for causing her husband stress.

Suffragettes wanted the right to vote. They wanted the president's support. They marched. They protested. They carried signs. They did this in front of the White House. They did this every day. They did this for months.

Mrs. Wilson supported her country. She just didn't support the suffragettes.

Explained by SCIENCE

A stroke happens when blood doesn't get to the brain. Blood vessels could be blocked. They could burst. They could leak. This stops air from getting to the brain. This kills brain cells. Brains control everything. Without blood, the brain will shut down. Strokes happen very quickly. There are different types of strokes. Strokes affect different parts of the brain. They affect brain tissues. FAST is a quick way to remember the effects of strokes. F stands for face dropping. A stands for arm weakness. S stands for speech difficulty. T stands for time to call 911. Strokes can also cause headaches. They can make people dizzy. People may have a hard time walking or moving. They may have a hard time eating. Strokes can affect people's vision. People may have trouble seeing. Strokes can confuse people. People may not understand things.

"I myself never made a single decision regarding the disposition of public affairs." – Edith Wilson

President Wilson had them taken to jail. This happened in 1917. Mrs. Wilson thought the suffragettes were "disgusting." She called them "devils in the **workhouse**." Workhouses were jails. Mrs. Wilson thought the suffragettes should stay in jail until they quit fighting.

The suffragettes were treated badly. They were beaten. They lived in dirty rooms. This bothered President Wilson. He changed his mind. He supported the 19th **Amendment**. Amendments are changes to laws. The 19th Amendment gave women the right to vote.

Edith Wilson died on December 28, 1961—on Woodrow Wilson's birthday.

After the president died, Mrs. Wilson spent the rest of her life protecting his good name. His last word before he died was "Edith."

Timeline

1872: Edith was born. She was born at 9:00 a.m. Her dad was a judge. He was late to court. He said that Edith started her life by "keeping gentlemen waiting."

1887: Edith briefly attended Martha Washington College.

1889: Edith attended Powell's School in Richmond.

1896: Edith married Norman Galt. Galt was a cousin of her older sister's husband.

1903: Edith Wilson had a son. Her son died.

1908: Galt died. Edith was left in charge of the business.

1915: Edith met President Wilson. They married. She became First Lady.

1917: Mrs. Wilson became the first honorary president of the Girl Scouts. Honorary means in name only. Mrs. Wilson started a tradition for future First Ladies.

1919: Mrs. Wilson attended the Paris Peace Conference. She went with President Wilson. She was the first First Lady to be involved with international diplomacy. Diplomacy is the work of keeping a good relationship between different countries.

1921: Mrs. Wilson left the White House. She and President Wilson moved into their home in Washington, D.C.

1924: Mrs. Wilson led the Women's National Democratic Club.

1939: Mrs. Wilson published her memoir. Memoirs are books about a person's life.

1941: Mrs. Wilson went to Congress with President Franklin D. Roosevelt. Roosevelt was asking for a declaration of war. This was after Pearl Harbor was attacked.

1961: Mrs. Wilson attended the inauguration of President John F. Kennedy. Inaugurations are when officials take office. This was Mrs. Wilson's last public appearance.

1961: Mrs. Wilson died. She died on the same day as President Wilson's birthday. She was supposed to be at the opening of the Woodrow Wilson Bridge. She was going to be the guest of honor.

Consider This!

Take a Position! The Constitution has amendments. The 25th Amendment sets out a plan for transfer of power. The vice president takes over if something happens to the president. But this didn't happen with President Wilson. Edith Wilson took over instead. Learn more about the 25th Amendment. Learn more about why Vice President Thomas R. Marshall didn't take over. Did Edith Wilson violate the Constitution? Argue your point with reasons and evidence.

Say What? Read the 45th Parallel Press book about Dolley Madison. Compare Dolley Madison to Edith Wilson. They were both First Ladies. Explain how they're alike. Explain how they're different.

Think About It! What do you think about a woman being the U.S. president? Research five female world leaders. Why do other countries have more female leaders than the United States?

Learn More

Ashby, Ruth. *Woodrow & Edith Wilson.* Milwaukee, WI: World Almanac Library, 2005.

Flanagan, Alice K. *Edith Bolling Galt Wilson.* New York: Children's Press, 1998.

Krull, Kathleen, and Anna Divito (illustr.). *A Kid's Guide to America's First Ladies.* New York: Harper, 2017.

Wells, Peggy Sue. *Edith Wilson.* Kennett Square, PA: Purple Toad Publishing, 2016.

Glossary

amendment (uh-MEND-muhnt) a change to the law that becomes law

democracy (dih-MOK-ruh-see) system of government in which people exercise their power by voting

descendants (dih-SEN-duhnts) people related to people who lived in the past

First Lady (FURST LAY-dee) title given to the wife of a male U.S. president

hostesses (HOH-stis-iz) women who host parties and events

license (LYE-suhns) a permit

ration (RASH-uhn) to save

shortage (SHOR-tij) a situation where there is not enough of something

steward (STOO-erd) caregiver

stroke (STROHK) a brain attack

suffragettes (suhf-ruh-JETS) women who fight for voting rights for women

war bond (WOR BAHND) money raised by the government to pay for wars

widower (WID-oh-er) a man whose spouse or partner died

workhouse (WURK-hous) jail

Index

First Ladies, 4, 5, 6, 10

Galt, Norman, 18–20

Lodge, Henry Cabot, 21

Pocahontas, 14, 16

stroke, 6, 21, 28
suffragettes, 26–29

Wilson, Edith
   family, 14–17
   first husband, 18–20
   as First Lady, 4, 5, 6, 10
   gets driver's license, 20
   meets and marries Woodrow, 22–25
   play about, 13
   as secret president, 6–9
   and suffragettes, 26–29
   timeline, 30
   and World War 1, 10–12

Wilson, Woodrow, 4
   meets and marries Edith, 22–25
   suffers stroke, 6–9, 21
women, 4, 26–29
World War I, 4, 10–12

About the Author

Dr. Virginia Loh-Hagan is an author, university professor, and former classroom teacher. Her dog, Woody, is named after her husband's granddad, Woody. Granddad Woody is named after President Woodrow Wilson. She lives in San Diego with her very tall husband and very naughty dogs. To learn more about her, visit www.virginialoh.com.